TIM FREKE is pioneering a new approach to spiritual awakening that has touched the hearts and minds of hundreds of thousands of people worldwide. He is the bestselling author of more than 30 books, which have been translated into 15 languages. He presents life-changing events internationally and online, during which he shares the experience of oneness and limitless love that naturally arises when we live lucidly.

For more information, videos and guided meditations visit www.TimFreke.com

LUCID LIVING
T!M FREKE

This is a revised version of Lucid Living published in 2016 by Watkins, an imprint of Watkins Media Limited.
19 Cecil Court
London WC2N 4EZ
enquiries@watkinspublishing.com

Managing Editor: Deborah Hercun
Editor: James Hodgson
Design: Barnaby Adams

A CIP record for this book is available from the British Library

ISBN: 978-1-78028-962-5

Set in Conduit and Myriad Pro

Printed and bound in Finland

www.watkinspublishing.com

LUCID LIVING

EXPERIENCE YOUR LIFE LIKE A LUCID DREAM

T!M FREKE

WATKINS

Sharing Wisdom Since
1893

Imagine for a moment you are dreaming.

You are completely engrossed in the dramas of your dream-world when a mysterious stranger appears in your dream. He sidles up to you and softly whispers something extraordinary in your ear. "Psst! Wake up. You're dreaming."

You are disconcerted but keep your cool. You know that the best way to deal with people who are clearly out-of-the-box is to nod politely and hope they'll go away. But the stranger is persistent. "I know it sounds mad to you right now, but you're dreaming."

You feel irritated. "That's absurd!"

The stranger is unperturbed. "Is it really absurd? Haven't you noticed how full of significant patterns and strange coincidences your experience is? As if there is some hidden meaning? Well, that's because this is a dream."

You become angry. "What! Are you saying that this world is just some kind of unreal delusion? I find that offensive. Tell that to all those people who are suffering!"

The stranger is patient. "Of course this world is real. It is a real dream-world. Its wonders are truly wonderful and its horrors are truly horrible. I'm not dismissing it. I'm simply pointing out that it's a dream."

You are confused. "What do you mean?"

The stranger explains. "Right now you think you are a person talking to me. But that's just who you temporarily appear to be in this dream. The real you is the dreamer. And this whole dream-world exists in you."

You feel stunned. "Are you asking me to believe that I am imagining talking to you? Surely you are not a product of my imagination?!"

The stranger smiles kindly. "The person that you seem to be is not imagining this conversation with me, because that person is a part of the dream. But really you are the dreamer who is imagining everything and everyone in this dream. We appear to be separate people having a conversation, but actually we are both the dreamer."

You begin to panic. "Now you're freaking me out. I'm losing my hold on who I am."

The stranger is reassuring. "Don't worry. You're just beginning to wake up. This is a dream of awakening. It is designed to make you progressively more conscious, until you're conscious enough to realise that you're dreaming."

You are confused. "But I don't understand. How do I wake up?"

The stranger looks you straight in the eye. "You can wake up anytime you want. You simply have to want to wake up more than you fear it. And there is nothing to fear. Waking up feels good. Knowing you are dreaming is the secret of enjoying the dream."

Your anxiety becomes excitement. You want to wake up. And the more you want to wake up the more you become conscious that you are dreaming. And that feels good.

You are no longer frightened of all the terrors that may afflict you in the dream, because you know that the 'real you' is safe. Even if the person you seem to be were to die it would be OK, because actually you are the dreamer.

Overwhelmed with gratitude you begin to thank the stranger, but he has moved on and is now deep in conversation with someone else, who is looking shocked and intrigued.

You call after him. "What now?"

He turns to you briefly and grins. "Enjoy the dream. And help everyone else to enjoy it as well, because we are all you."

For a moment you just stand there and let this awesome realisation sink in. Then you notice nearby a number of anxious-looking people hurrying about their business, fully convinced they know exactly who they are and what is going on. You smile to yourself, sidle up to one of them and whisper softly …

"Psst! Wake up. You're dreaming."

Wouldn't that be an amazing dream! But how would you react if this actually were to happen to you right now?

Because I am the stranger and I want to make an extraordinary suggestion …

Life is not what it seems.

You are not who you think you are.

Life is like a dream and you are the dreamer.

Have you ever been conscious that you were dreaming while asleep at night? This is known as 'lucid dreaming'. I want to suggest that it is possible to experience an ultra-awake state I call 'lucid living', in which you are conscious that life is like a dream right now.

But I'm not asking you to just believe me. I want to share with you a way of thinking about life that will wake you up, so that you experience lucid living for yourself.

Lucid living requires a fundamental shift of perspective, comparable to looking at one of those pictures of coloured dots that suddenly turn into a spectacular 3D image.

The first such picture I looked at promised me dolphins, but I could see only dots. I didn't know how to make the image come alive. My friends kept assuring me that, if I just stopped concentrating on the dots and focused my eyes on infinity instead, I would definitely see the 3D image. But the more I was reassured, the more irritated I became at my failure.

Then suddenly, for a startling moment, the magic happened. Dots became dolphins, leaping life-like out of the page towards me. And, just as suddenly, they were gone again. Encouraged by my brief success, I kept looking until I gradually got it. Now I can see these 3D images quite easily.

Experiencing lucid living can be like this. At first it sounds ludicrous, but keep looking and eventually you will get it. The trick to viewing a 3D image is to change your visual focus. The trick to experiencing lucid living is to change the way you think.

And that is what I am here to help you do. I want to introduce you to a way of thinking about life that will utterly transform your experience of living.

I feel privileged that you have invited me into your mind to share these ideas with you.
And I don't want to abuse your hospitality by wasting any of your valuable time. So I've kept things as concise as possible, by distilling down the simple essence of lucid philosophy.

But that makes for rich reading, which means this book needs to be savoured not gulped. Speed-reading may lead to mental indigestion. The more consciously you read, the more likely you are to experience lucid living.

I am going to lead you through eight powerful insights that will work together to wake you up from the sleeping sickness that keeps you unconscious in the life-dream.

Some of these insights are deceptively simple. Some may seem familiar and others may seem weird. But I urge you to approach each insight with an open mind and to give it your undivided attention. If you assume you already understand what a particular insight means, or you have already decided that it's meaningless nonsense, this can prevent you awakening.

To help you avoid just reading the words and missing the meaning of each insight, I am going to suggest you perform a number of philosophical experiments. In these experiments I will talk you into experiencing lucid living by posing questions and then presenting my answers.

Take the time to perform each experiment yourself and see if my answers also work for you. Make sure you actually do this. Otherwise lucid living will remain just a bizarre idea.

Before we embark on our philosophical adventure, let me make something very clear. When I compare life to a dream I do not mean to denigrate it as some sort of meaningless fantasy. Life is too wonderful to be called an illusion, unless we whisper the word in amazement, as we might when witnessing the most astonishing magic trick.

What could be more magnificent than this glorious universe, in all its multifarious extravagance, its awesome vastness and delicate detail, its impersonal precision and intimate intensity, its harsh necessities and lush sensuality? Lucid living is realising how marvellous life really is.

This is a little book with grand aspirations.
It will take you less than an hour to read, but it
could change your life for good.

I urge you to read it straight through, because
you're more likely to reach a philosophical
climax if you take it in all at once. Especially if
it is your first time.

I can't promise to wake you up. Lucid living
is like falling in love. It happens when it
happens. You can't force it and you can't
prevent it.

But I can take you on a blind date with
some extremely bold and beautiful ideas.
And – you never know – it might be the
beginning of something big!

So let me introduce our first insight …

LIFE IS A MYSTERY

The idea that life is like a dream seems preposterous because we presume we are already wide awake. But most of the time we are so unconscious we don't even notice the most obvious thing about existence – it is an enigma of mind-boggling enormity.

Life is the mother of all mysteries – quite literally! Yet we are normally so asleep that we manage to go about our daily business as if being alive is nothing remarkable.

Join me in a philosophical experiment and let's examine the human predicament …

Here we are.

Meeting in this perpetual moment we call 'now'.

Participants in this bizarre business we call 'life'.

Awaiting the inevitable ending we call 'death'.

What's it all about?!

Do you know?

Does anyone really know?

People travel all over the world in search of mysteries and miracles, but what could be more mysterious and miraculous than life itself?

Not just what it is, but that it is at all!

When the Hubble Space Telescope was focused on the night sky, each tiny black dot revealed dozens of galaxies, with each galaxy containing billions of stars!

The universe is too immense to imagine and infinitely mysterious. And if you live to be eighty years old you will have around 4,000 weeks in which to understand it.

That puts things in perspective, don't you think?

Our predicament is so profoundly puzzling it is astonishing that we aren't permanently perplexed.

Most of us rush around as if there is no more to life than making a living and not thinking about dying.

We never stop to wonder.

We behave as if we know exactly what life is all about, even though secretly we know that we don't.

It is as if we are mesmerised by our assumptions about life into a semi-conscious trance, which anaesthetises us to the awesome strangeness of existence.

That is until the bubble bursts and we unexpectedly wake up.

It may be an encounter with death that jolts us back to life. Or the bewildering bliss of falling in love. Or a simple shaft of sunlight through a window.

Whatever form the wake-up call takes, for a marvellous moment we shake off the numbness we call 'normality' and find ourselves immersed in overwhelming, unfathomable, breathtaking mystery.

Have you ever had an experience like this?

The fact that we normally take life for granted, when it is actually so utterly mysterious, shows how unconscious we usually are.

We are so wrapped up in our opinions about life that we mistake our own make-believe world for reality – just as when we are dreaming.

Become conscious of the mystery of existence right now – and it will feel like waking up from a dream.

If you're feeling mystified, that's good, because it means you're ready for our second insight …

NOW IS ALL
YOU KNOW

When we dream, things are not what they seem. We are so engrossed in our imagination that we don't realise we are dreaming. We believe we know what is going on, but really we don't.

I want to suggest that life is like a dream and that right now we are so engrossed in the life-dream that we don't realise we are dreaming. We believe we know what is going on, but really we don't.

Most of us assume our everyday understanding of life is right. But can we really be so certain? I want to suggest that all we actually know for sure is what we are experiencing right now. And if we really pay attention to our experience of this moment we will discover that life is like a dream.

Join me in another philosophical experiment and let's think it through together …

To most people the idea that life is like a dream is ludicrous.

I'm a philosopher not an evangelist, so I am all in favour of giving new ideas a sceptical reception.

But I am also in favour of adopting the same sceptical attitude towards our familiar ideas.

Are you open to the possibility that your present understanding of life could be mistaken?

Is there anything about which you can be absolutely certain?

Can you be certain of the common-sense understanding of reality taken for granted by most people in our culture?

I don't think so.

History shows that today's sensible certainties

soon become tomorrow's silly superstitions. We look back at many of the beliefs of our ancestors and find them crazy and amusing. Isn't it possible that our descendants will look back at our present cultural assumptions and find them equally crazy and amusing?

Can you be certain of your own personal convictions?

I don't think so.

Haven't you often felt completely sure about something, only to decide later that you were wrong. Isn't it possible you will discover your present beliefs are also wrong?

Are you with me?

You can doubt all the beliefs that you have taken on trust from other people, because you don't know them to be true for yourself.

Do you agree?

You can doubt all beliefs that are based on your memories of the past, because memory is fallible.

That's a full-on thought, but it's right, isn't it?

Is there anything about which you can be absolutely certain?

Yes.

You are experiencing something right now.

That's indisputably true, isn't it?

Your experience of this moment is not a belief that can be questioned. It is a self-evident certainty.

Your experience of this moment is all you can be absolutely sure of.

So, the only way to really understand life is to examine your own immediate experience of living.

Isn't that an empowering realisation!

If you want to know what is going on, you can't rely on me or anyone else to tell you.

You must find out for yourself by paying attention to what you are experiencing right now.

And – I want to suggest – if you do become more conscious of this present moment, you will discover that life is like a dream.

OK so far? Because from here it's a bit of a philosophical roller-coaster ride. Hang on tight. Or better still let go completely! Because we are going to be moving fast.

Lucid living isn't believing the theory that life is like a dream. It is directly experiencing the dream-like nature of reality in this present moment.

I want to point out some clues which suggest life is like a dream so that you can check them out for yourself in your own immediate experience.

The first clue is our next insight. But be prepared – it challenges our most basic assumption about who we are …

YOU ARE NOT
A PERSON

When you are dreaming you appear to be a character within the dream. But this is only your 'apparent identity'. It is who you appear to be, but not who you really are. Essentially you are awareness dreaming the dream. This is your 'essential identity'.

I am suggesting that life is like a dream. Right now you appear to be a person in the life-dream. But this is only your 'apparent identity', it is not who you really are. Your 'essential identity' is much less concrete and much more mysterious. You are awareness witnessing the life-dream.

Take a look with me …

You are experiencing something right now.

That's obvious, right?

So you are an experiencer of experiences.

That may be an unfamiliar way of describing yourself, but it's clearly true, isn't it?

Become conscious of being the 'experiencer' of this moment and let's explore what that means.

The 'experiencer' is your essential identity which you call 'I'.

The 'I' is witnessing everything you are seeing, hearing, touching and imagining.

Can you get that?

The 'I' is aware of an ever-changing stream of experiences right now.

But what is the 'I'?

Is the 'I' your body?

No. The body is something you are experiencing. It isn't the experiencer.

Is the 'I' your mind?

No. The mind is something you are experiencing. It isn't the experiencer.

The 'I' is aware of everything you are experiencing, so the 'I' could be called 'awareness'.

That may sound a strange way of describing your identity – but try it out.

Be awareness experiencing this moment.

Common sense says you are a person. But even in everyday speech we say 'I have a body', not 'I am a body'. And we talk of 'my mind' as if the mind is something we possess, not something we are.

This is because the 'I' is not the body or mind.

The 'I' is awareness witnessing the body and mind.

Can you get that?

Over your lifetime your body has aged and your mind has matured, but don't you feel as if something has remained the same?

Isn't the essential 'you' no different now from when you were much younger?

What is this essential 'you' that is constant and enduring?

It is awareness.

Awareness is the constant background of all your experiences.

Awareness is the unchanging witness of all that changes.

Awareness is a perpetual presence that is always present.

Do you agree?

Right now you are awareness witnessing a stream of experiences. This is your permanent essential identity.

Within the stream of experiences you appear to be a particular person. This is your ever-changing apparent identity.

Your apparent identity is not who you essentially are. It is who you temporarily appear to be.

This will become obvious if you consider your experience of waking and dreaming.

When you dream at night, the person you presently appear to be disappears from awareness and you appear to be a different person in a different dream-world.

Your essential identity as awareness remains the same, but your apparent identity is completely transformed every night.

Common sense says that you are the body that falls asleep and wakes each day.

But in your own experience you are awareness within which different bodies appear and disappear on a regular basis!

That's an outrageous thought, but it's right, isn't it?

While you are dreaming you believe you are the person you appear to be in the dream. But when you dream lucidly you realise you are much more than you seem to be, because you are the dreamer.

If you want to live lucidly you need to see that you are much more than you seem to be right now.

When you dream at night you are awareness witnessing a stream of experiences within which you appear to be a person.

Take a look at this moment – it is the same.

You are awareness witnessing a stream of experiences within which you appear to be a person.

How are you doing?

Grasping unfamiliar ideas can be a bit like trying to hold onto the soap in the bath, so take a mental breather if you need one.

But not too long, because we're working towards a reality-shift which will – quite literally – turn the world inside out.
And that will require plenty of philosophical momentum.

OK. Ready to play? Insight number four is …

THE WORLD
EXISTS IN YOU

In a dream you appear to be a dream-persona in a dream-world, but essentially you are awareness and the dream-world exists within you.

In the same way, right now you appear to be a person in the life-dream, but essentially you are awareness and the life-dream exists within you.

Let's examine the moment …

Right now you are experiencing your thoughts and the world of the senses.

Do you agree?

We usually think of our thoughts as existing within awareness and the world as existing independently of awareness. But is that right?

If you pay attention to what is happening right now you will see that you experience the world as a series of sensations: visual images, tactile feelings, background sounds, ambient aromas.

And sensations exist within awareness, don't they?

Everything you are aware of exists within awareness, otherwise you wouldn't be aware of it!

So what is awareness?

Awareness isn't something within your experience. It is an emptiness that contains all you are experiencing.

Is that true? Try it out and see how it feels.

Be the spacious emptiness of awareness within which everything you are experiencing exists.

These printed words you are reading on this page exist within awareness.

These ideas reverberating in your mind exist within awareness.

All you see and hear and touch and imagine exists within awareness.

Your body exists within awareness.

The world exists within awareness.

You may appear to be a body in the world, but essentially you are awareness and the world exists in you – just like when you are dreaming.

If that comes as a shock, there's more.

You don't exist in time!

Look for yourself right now.

Time is the perpetual flow of ever-changing appearances that awareness witnesses.

Time exists within awareness.

Awareness is outside of time.

You are timeless awareness dreaming itself to be a person in time.

Are you suffering from philosophical vertigo?

Well, stay steady, because our fifth insight is a very big idea indeed …

ALL IS ONE

When we dream we appear to be one of many characters in the dream-drama. However, everyone and everything in the dream is being imagined by one dreaming awareness.

I want to suggest it is the same right now. We appear to be many separate individuals. However, we are all different characters in the life-dream that is being dreamt by the one life-dreamer.

Let's explore this together …

As a person you have different mental and physical characteristics from me.

Do you agree?

Your apparent identity is distinct from my apparent identity, but is your essential identity as awareness distinct from my essential identity as awareness?

Examine the reality of this moment and think it through with me.

Awareness can't be touched, because it has no shape.

Awareness can't be seen, because it has no colour.

Awareness can't be heard, because it makes no noise.

Awareness is a formless presence, which has no boundaries.

So how can your essential nature as awareness be separate from my essential nature as awareness?

You are formless awareness that exists outside of space and time … and so am I.

Can you get that?

As awareness we are one, but what we are experiencing is different.

So try out this possibility and see how it feels.

We are formless awareness dreaming itself to be many individuals with different experiences in the life-dream.

We appear to be separate, but essentially we are one.

Are you enjoying the ride?

Don't be surprised to find yourself feeling like Neo in *The Matrix* or Alice in *Through the Looking-Glass,* because in a way you are. Except the life-story is even more full of ironic twists.

Lucid living is realising you are both the hero of your particular story and the imagination that is conceiving the whole cosmic drama.

It is understanding our sixth insight …

YOU ARE A
PARADOX

When you dream, you are both the source of the dream and a character within the dream. Your identity is inherently paradoxical. In the same way, your identity right now is also inherently paradoxical. You are both the source of the life-dream and a character within it.

You are the life-dreamer imagining yourself to be a particular person in the life-dream. While you identify exclusively with your life-persona you will remain unconsciously engrossed in the life-dream. Lucid living happens when you become conscious of both poles of your paradoxical nature.

Give it a go …

You appear to be a body in the world.

Now flip it around.

You are awareness and the world exists in you.

Try it again …

You appear to be a person in time.

Flip it around.

You are a permanent presence witnessing an ever-changing flow of appearances.

Try it again …

You appear to be a separate individual.

Flip it around.

You are the life-dreamer experiencing existence from a particular point of view.

One more time …

You appear to be a character in the life-dream.

Flip it around.

You are the life-dreamer and everything is you.

Lucid living is consciously being all that you are.

Waking up to the oneness of your essential identity doesn't negate your individuality.

Quite the opposite.

Lucid living is understanding just how important your individuality is, because it is by dreaming itself to be you as an individual that the life-dreamer is able to experience the life-dream.

Lucid living doesn't deny the delights and dramas of everyday existence. It charges them with new significance and meaning.

Everything you experience is a manifestation of your essential identity. So everything is showing you something about who you are – like a dream.

You are continually dreaming up new situations to give yourself the opportunity to become more conscious.

Do you know what I mean?

Waking up doesn't mean withdrawing from life and becoming detached. Quite the opposite.

It means wholeheartedly engaging with the life-dream as an amazing adventure of self-discovery.

We have travelled a huge distance in a short time, so don't be surprised to feel a little dizzy with philosophical jetlag.

Yet here we are, exactly where we started. Conscious of this present moment.

Nothing has changed. Yet everything has changed, because waking up fundamentally transforms how it feels to be a person in the life-dream.

And this brings us to the climax of our philosophical reality-check. Insight number seven is …

BEING ONE
IS LOVING ALL

What is love? It seems to me that love is how oneness feels. We love someone when we are so close we connect through the separateness that seems to divide us.

Normally we presume we are just the person we appear to be, so we feel connected to those we embrace within this limited sense of who we are, such as our friends and family.
We are hostile to those who threaten our personal self and indifferent to everyone else. Our loving stops where our sense of self ceases.

But when we realise we are essentially one with everyone and everything, we find ourselves intimately connected to everyone and everything. We experience love without limits.

Check it out …

Meet me in this moment.

These words are reaching through time and space connecting us together.

I am conscious of you reading. Are you conscious of me writing?

Here we are.

The one life-dreamer meeting itself in different forms.

Apparently separate. Essentially the same.

Are you with me?

How does it feel to realise that we are not separate?

How does it feel to be one with everyone and everything?

For me it is an experience of communion and compassion.

Being one with all, I am in love with all.

When I wake up to oneness I feel a limitless love which is so deep and poignant it embraces life in all its ecstasy and agony.

I share in our collective joy and suffering. And I find my selfish preoccupations are replaced by a longing for everyone to love living.

When I know I am the life-dreamer I want to enjoy the life-dream in all my many disguises.

I want to alleviate our collective distress, so that we can celebrate the miracle of existence together – without fear, oppression and hardship.

Don't you also want that?

Since time immemorial wise men and women have been assuring us that love is the only solution to our problems – and they are right.

Only love can heal the divisions between us, because love is the realisation that we are one.

When we assume we are just separate individuals we act in our limited self-interest, regardless of the suffering we may cause others.

Being lost in separateness leads to selfishness and suffering.

But becoming conscious of oneness leads to the selfless desire to create universal wellbeing.

When we see through separateness we understand that conflict is never between us and them, but always us against us.

This realisation has huge implications.

It means harming others is hurting ourselves.

It means revenge – even against the most hideous criminals – is hurting ourselves again.

It means war – no matter how righteous – is grotesque self-mutilation.

Can you see all the needless harm we are causing ourselves through our mistaken belief that we are separate.

Now imagine how easily we could utterly transform our collective experience of life if we simply lived lucidly in love with all.

Imagine for a moment how good the life-dream would be if we could just wake up!

Lucid living is the simple secret of transforming the life-dream from a nightmare of separateness into the joyous celebration of existence we want it to be.

Thank you for coming with me on this mind trip into the mystery of the moment.

I hope the experience of waking up is as exhilarating for you as it is for me.

Our eighth insight is my parting gift …

YOU ARE THE ONE

People have been waking up and living lucidly throughout history. It is a natural state that has been written about at all times in all cultures.

Sometimes when people talk about awakening they describe the dream of life as a pernicious illusion we need to escape, but that doesn't feel right to me.

The more I dissolve into the oneness, the more animated I feel as a unique individual. The more I feel filled with limitless love, the more I long to share it. The more I wake up, the more precious this dream of life becomes to me.

So this is my heartfelt message to you, dear friend …

You are the life-dreamer dreaming the dream of you.

It is an amazing, transformative, bittersweet dream, full of laughter and tears, triumphs and losses, hope and despair.

If you give yourself to this great dream it will awaken you to what-is.

If you consciously engage with this deep drama it will teach you kindness and make you wise.

So why not dare to commit to the adventure of your life?

Because essentially you are always safe, even when the life-dream becomes a nightmare.

That's right, isn't it?

When you dream it can be terrifying, but if you dream lucidly you know you are always

essentially safe, because you're not just the person you appear to be in the dream.
You are the dreamer.

In the same way, if you live lucidly there is a deep knowing that you are always essentially safe.

So take the risk and really live!

You are the one appearing as someone and your life is deeply significant.

You are the one who can light up the darkness.

You are the one who can bring love to your world.

You are the one you've been waiting for.

I am writing these words to wake you up, because I see what a wonder you are.

You are infinite potential playing at being a person.

The creativity that created the whole universe is within you and it wants to express itself through you.

Can you hear the call to share your gifts with the world?

You are the mystery of life made manifest.

I am in awe of your vastness and touched by your fragility.

I see your greatness and your smallness – and I celebrate both.

I encourage you to wake up to oneness and feel the limitless love, so you can embrace your vulnerable, tender, ambiguous humanity – just as it is.

I embrace you as you are.

I reach out to you.

You are different from me and yet we are one.

And it is only because we are both separate and the same that we can love one another.

That's beautiful!

I want you to see yourself as I see you.

So that we can help each other to make this journey of life.

So that we can inspire each other when we feel lucid and in love.

And comfort each other when we feel lost and alone.

So that we can walk each other home.

So that when I forget and fall asleep into life, you can remind me of the possibility of living lucidly.

You may be that kind stranger who will sidle up and whisper softly …

"Psst! Wake up. You're dreaming."

TRANSFORMATIVE EVENTS

If you want to continue our journey together I invite you to join me at one of my transformative events. There's a magic that happens when we're present in the same place, so come and dive into the deep love with me. It would be wonderful to spend some personal time with you.

You can find information on my website www.TimFreke.com

MORE BOOKS BY TIM FREKE

DEEP AWAKE
Wake up to oneness and become a lover of life

THE MYSTERY EXPERIENCE
A revolutionary approach to spiritual awakening

HOW LONG IS NOW?
How to be spiritually awake in the real world

These and many more of Tim's books are available from www.TimFreke.com

GRATITUDE

This book would not exist without
the generous support of Sean Reynolds,
Angie Hayward, Debbie O'Shea Freke,
Des Rice, Tony Taylor and Barnaby Adams.

Thank you. I love you.

WATKINS

Sharing Wisdom Since
1893

The story of Watkins Publishing dates back to March 1893, when John M. Watkins, a scholar of esotericism, overheard his friend and teacher Madame Blavatsky lamenting the fact that there was nowhere in London to buy books on mysticism, occultism or metaphysics. At that moment Watkins was born, soon to become the home of many of the leading lights of spiritual literature, including Carl Jung, Rudolf Steiner, Alice Bailey and Chögyam Trungpa.

Today our passion for vigorous questioning is still resolute. With over 350 titles on our list, Watkins Publishing reflects the development of spiritual thinking and new science over the past 120 years. We remain at the cutting edge, committed to publishing books that change lives.

DISCOVER MORE ...

Read our blog

Watch and listen to
our authors in action

Sign up to
our mailing list

JOIN IN THE CONVERSATION

WatkinsPublishing   @watkinswisdom

WatkinsPublishingLtd   +watkinspublishing1893

Our books celebrate conscious, passionate, wise and happy living.
Be part of the community by visiting

www.watkinspublishing.com